DON'T
GIVE A FIG

First published in Great Britain in 2019 by Pyramid,
an imprint of Octopus Publishing Group Ltd, a Hachette
UK Company.

Don't Give a Fig.
Copyright © 2019 by Octopus Publishing Group Ltd.

Published in 2020 by
Harper Design
An Imprint of HarperCollinsPublishers
195 Broadway
New York, New York 10007
Tel: (212) 207-7000
Fax: (855) 746-6023
harperdesign@harpercollins.com
www.hc.com

Distributed throughout North America by
HarperCollins Publishers
195 Broadway
New York, New York 10007

ISBN 978-0-06-299521-6
Library of Congress Control Number has been applied for.

Printed in Singapore
First Printing, 2020

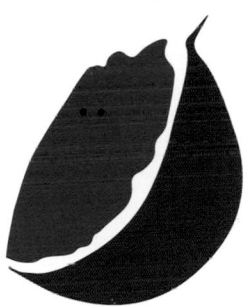

DON'T
GIVE A FIG

words of wisdom for when
life gives you lemons

To: ....

From: ....

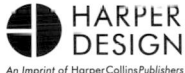

HARPER
DESIGN

An Imprint of HarperCollins Publishers

NO PAIN
NO GRAIN

ASPARAGUS THE DETAILS, IT'S
THYME TO MOVE ON

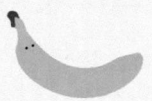

WHEN LIFE GIVES YOU LEMONS,
MAKE LIKE A BANANA AND SPLIT

DON'T LET IT
RYEL YOU UP

DRAW A LIME IN
THE SAND AND LET
NO ONE CROSS IT

NEVER AGRAIN

IT'S NO BIG DILL

IT WAS THYME FOR A CHANGE ANYWAY

RICE UP!

I SAID TOMAYTO,
HE SAID TOMAHTO,
SO I SAID FIG OFF

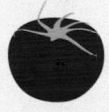

CHOI TO THE WORLD!

LET THAT SHIITAKE GO

"Near, far, wherever you are, I believe that the artichoke does go on"

CELINE DION

REZEST MUCH

OBEY LITTLE

DON'T LET IT GET

JALAPENO BUSINESS

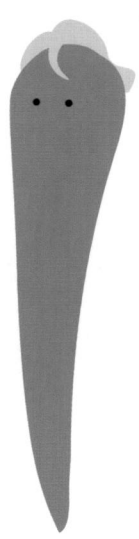

KALE SERA, SERA

WHEN YOU FEEL LIKE
YOU HAVEN'T BEAN
CURD, SHOUT LOUDER

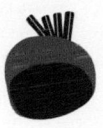

ALWAYS BEETROOT TO YOURSELF
BECAUSE THERE ARE VERY FEW PEOPLE
WHO WILL ALWAYS BEETROOT TO YOU

"LIVE AS IF YOU WERE TO DIE TOMARROW"

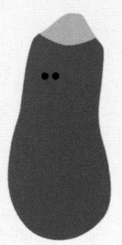

GANDHI

BROCCOLEAVE ME THE HELL ALONE

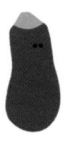

LEARN FROM YESTERDAY
LIVE FOR TODAY
HOPE FOR TOMARROW

"PAPRIKA DON'T PREACH"

MADONNA

AIN'T NOBODY GOT THYME FOR THAT

LET'S
TAKE THIS
SPROUTSIDE

"CHIA-CHIA-CHIA-CHIA-CHANGES"

DAVID BOWIE

#wejammin

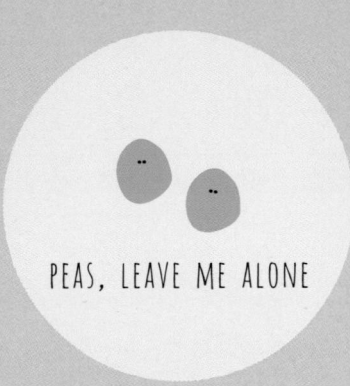

PEAS, LEAVE ME ALONE

YOU WALNUT BE BROKEN

PEANOUGH IS ENOUGH

HERE TODAY,
TARRAGON TOMORROW

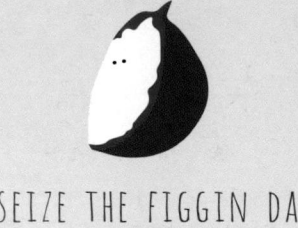

SEIZE THE FIGGIN DAY

GO CARPE THE SHIITAKE OUT OF THIS DIEM

YOU WANNA PEACH OF ME, BEETS?

JUST BEET IT

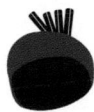

TOMARROW IS ANOTHER DAY

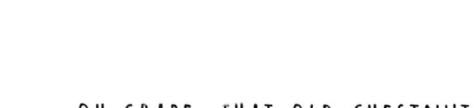

OH GRAPE, THAT OLD CHESTNUT

DO WHAT MATTERS.

FIGET THE REST

KEEP YOUR FRIENDS CLOSE AND YOUR ENDIVES CLOSER

EVERY DAY YOU'RE BRUSSELIN

REVENGE
IS SWEDE

#youokalehun

SHIITAKE HAPPENS

DON'T GIVE A DAMSON

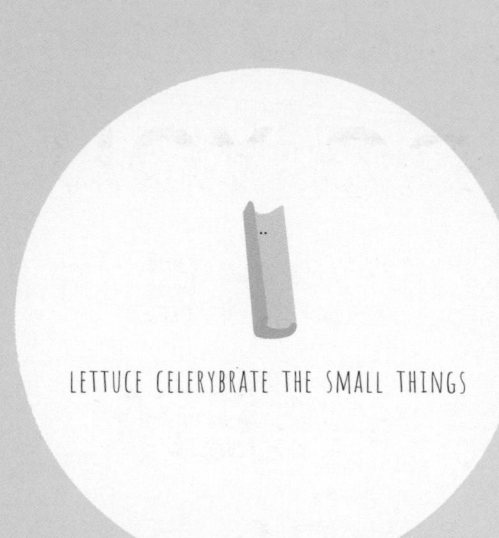

LETTUCE CELERYBRATE THE SMALL THINGS

HOW DO YOU LIKE THEM APPLES?

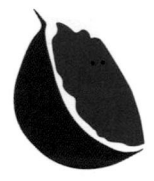

JUST BE YOU,
AND IF PEOPLE DON'T
LIKE IT, WELL, FIG 'EM

YOU DON'T NEED ANYONE'S PERSIMMON

PEAS FIG OFF

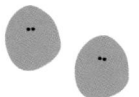

GO, MAN GO!

IT TAKES TWO TO MANGO

GET RID OF YOUR
EXCESS CABBAGE

DON'T LET LIFE
BEET YOU DOWN

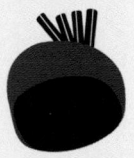

#likaleyeah

BEAN THERE,

DONE THAT,

GOT THE PEA SHIRT

IT'S NOT YOUR CRESS TO BEAR

REMEMBER, YOU ALWAYS
HAVE A CHOYS

You're
as dramatic
as a soap okra

#beetdown

NEVER PUT THE KIWI
TO YOUR HAPPINESS IN
SOMEBODY ELSE'S POCKET

KILL THEM WITH SUCCESS, BERRY THEM WITH A SMILE

"BLIND BAYLEAF

IS DANGEROUS"

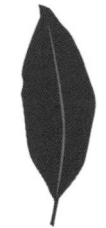

PROVERB

WHAT DOESN'T
KALE YOU MAKES
YOU STRONGER

PEACH,
DON'T KILL
MY VIBE

IT AIN'T OVER LENTIL IT'S OVER

HATERS GONNA HATE.
Potataoes gonna potate

GIVE ME ONE
GOOD RAISIN WHY I
SHOULD FIGIVE YOU

DON'T
GRAIN
ON MY
PARADE

YOU CAN HAVE ANYTHING YOU
WANT IF YOU ARE WILLING TO
GIVE UP THE BAYLEAF THAT YOU
CAN'T HAVE 11

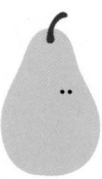

KEEP THINGS IN PEARSPECTIVE

FIGHT THE GOURD FIGHT

YOU ARE NOT PEARANOID

OH KALE
YOU WIN

IF THEY'RE SO
CHARD TO LOVE...

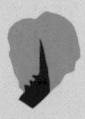

...LET THAT (wo)MANGO

KNOW YOUR LIMIT.

DO NOT CROSS THE LIME

IF LOOKS COULD KALE

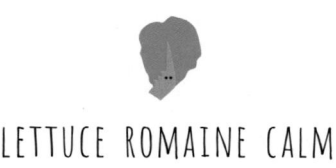

LETTUCE ROMAINE CALM

"IN MATTERS OF STYLE, SWIM WITH THE CURRANT. IN MATTERS OF PRINCIPLE, STAND LIKE A ROCK"

THOMAS JEFFERSON

TAKE IT SLOE

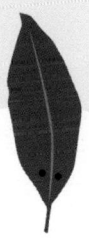

"BAYLEAF HAS THE POWER
TO CHANGE YOUR
INNER STATE AND YOUR
OUTER WORLD"

JOHN PAUL WARREN

WHATEVER HAPPENS, ROMAINE CALM

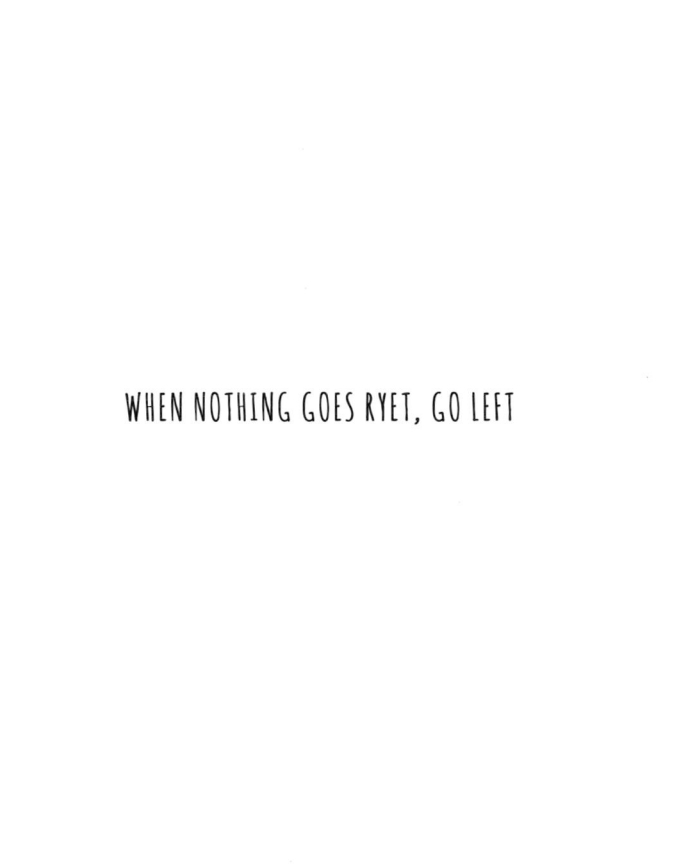

WHEN NOTHING GOES RYET, GO LEFT

"LORD DON'T SLOE ME DOWN"

OASIS

WHEN IN ROME,

DO AS THE ROMAINES DO

YOU'RE THE BOSS THAT CAN'T BE BEET

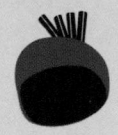

"OH GOURD WON'T YOU BUY ME A MERCEDES BENZ"

JANIS JOPLIN

YEAH YOU'VE GOT SASS.

THEY NEED TO DILL WITH IT

#dillbreaker

THIS IS BUILDING TO A CRESSENDO

GOOD THINGS

COME TO

THOSE WHO WHEAT

TATERS
GONNA TATE

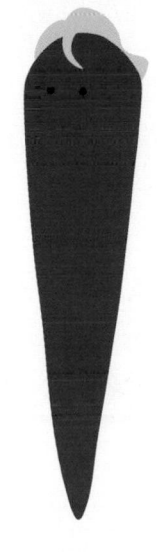

DON'T
CARROT ALL

#wheatever

For those of you who haven't herb enough, and haven't herb-it-all-bivore, this series has all the chiaing things you've ever wanted to say in vegan-friendly puns.*

Find the pearfect gift for any occasion:

AVOCUDDLE
comfort words for when you're feeling downbeet

YOU ARE 24 CARROT GOLD
words of love for someone who's worth their weight in root vegetables

I AM GRAPEFUL
all the good thymes I want to thank you for

*Or plant-based puns if, like us, you are no longer sure if avocados are vegan. Or friendly.

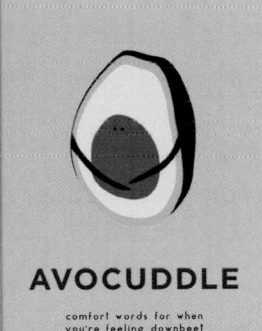

AVOCUDDLE

comfort words for when
you're feeling downbeet

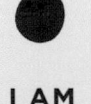

I AM
GRAPEFUL

all the good thymes I want to
thank you for

DILLON AND KALE SPROUTS

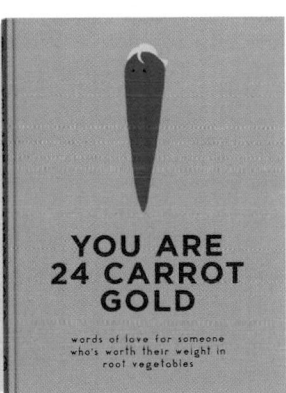

YOU ARE
24 CARROT
GOLD

words of love for someone
who's worth their weight in
root vegetables

Acknowledgments and Apologies

With thanks to Andrew, Anna, Steph and Matt for their contributions, and special thanks to Joe as his contributions were really quite good.

We regret not being able to say anything nice with cavolo nero, kohlrabi, sorrel and fenugreek.
We hold anyone who can in the highest regard.

"patience is bitter but its fruit is sweet"
Aristotle